Simple Solutions for a
Gluten and Dairy Free Diet

Joyce Ovens

Simple Solutions for a Gluten and Dairy Free Diet

iUniverse books may be ordered through booksellers or by contacting:

iUniverse
1663 Liberty Drive
Bloomington, IN 47403
www.iuniverse.com
1-800-Authors (1-800-288-4677)

Because of the dynamic nature of the Internet, any web addresses or links contained in this book may have changed since publication and may no longer be valid. The views expressed in this work are solely those of the author and do not necessarily reflect the views of the publisher, and the publisher hereby disclaims any responsibility for them.

Any people depicted in stock imagery provided by Getty Images are models, and such images are being used for illustrative purposes only. Certain stock imagery © Getty Images.

ISBN: 978-1-5320-7610-7 (sc)
ISBN: 978-1-5320-7611-4 (e)

Library of Congress Control Number: 2019906336

Print information available on the last page.

iUniverse rev. date: 06/07/2019

Acknowledgements: Love and thanks to my husband, Jim, photographer and typist.

In loving memory of a special

friend, Donna Garland.

Contents

1 Appetizers

a. Elegant Asparagus Appetizer

b. Roasted Red Pepper Hummus

c. Simple Appetizers

Elegant Asparagus Appetizer

Ingredients

1 lb	Asparagus
½	Red Onion
2 tbsp	Olives
1	Tomato
1 tbsp	Olive Oil
2 tbsp	Red Wine Vinegar
2 cloves	Garlic
2 tbsp	Honey

Directions

- Wash asparagus and steam for 4 minutes.
- Check with a fork to ensure that it is done.
- Dry on paper towel.
- Cut asparagus into approximately 1 inch pieces.
- Arrange asparagus on platter with thin slices of red onion.
- Blend tomato, chopped with skin, olive oil, cut up olives, red wine vinegar, minced garlic and honey.
- Set mixture in refrigerator for 1 hour.
- Then drizzle mixture over the asparagus.

Enjoy!

Note: ½ a white onion can replace the red onion, but the latter provides more colour. Olives can be omitted.

Elegant Asparagus Appetizer

Roasted Red Pepper Hummus

Ingredients

1 can	(540 ml)	Chickpeas, drained and rinsed
½ cup	(125 ml)	Chopped Roasted Red Peppers
¼ cup	(60 ml)	Tahini
2 tbsp	(25 ml)	Olive Oil
2 tbsp	(25 ml)	Water
1 tbsp	(15 ml)	Lemon Juice
¼ cup		Fresh Parsley
		Fresh Veggies or Pita for serving.

Directions

- Wash and remove seeds from the red pepper.
- Cut red pepper in strips and toss with olive oil.
- Place pepper on pan individually and roast at 400F for 10 minutes. If not done, leave in oven for 2-3 minutes longer.
- Wipe any remaining oil off the red pepper with a paper towel.
- In food processor, pulse together chickpeas, tahini, oil and water until very smooth. Pulse in lemon juice, fresh parsley and chopped red pepper.
- Serve hummus with fresh veggies or pita.

Note: Omit red pepper and use ½ cup of chopped roasted vegetables. Spices can be added such as 1 small garlic clove, minced or ½ tsp coriander. Adjust spices as desired.

Remaining hummus can be stored in an airtight container in the refrigerator for one week.

Roasted Red Pepper Hummus

Simple Appetizers
Avocado Dip

Ingredients

1	*Avocado*
1 bag	*Deep Blue and Flax Tortillas*

Directions

- Mash avocado.
- Use avocado or dip with the blue corn tortillas.

Fresh Vegetable Tray

Ingredients

1	*Zucchini*
1	*Carrot*
1	*Celery*
	Cherry Tomatoes
1	*Cucumber*
	Mushrooms
1	*Fresh Pepper, Green and/or Red*
½ Cup	*Hummus*

Directions

- Slice zucchini and cucumber.
- Peel carrots and cut into strips.
- Cut celery stalks into 3-4 in. sticks.
- Wash and dry mushrooms and cut into halves.
- Cut peppers into ¼ in strips.
- Add or delete whatever vegetables you prefer.
- Serve with Hummus.

2 Soups and Salads

Creamy Broccoli Soup
(Gluten Free)

Ingredients

2 Bunches	Broccoli
1 Tbsp	Extra-virgin Olive Oil
1 Large	Onion
1 or 2	Garlic Cloves
½ Tsp	Salt
¼ Tsp	Ground Pepper
2 Cups	Vegetable or Chicken Broth
½ Cup	Sugar Free Almond Milk
2 Tbsp	Fresh Lemon Juice

Directions

- Chop broccoli stems and florets.
- Finely chop the onion.
- Mince the garlic cloves.
- In a large saucepan, heat the olive oil over medium heat. Add the chopped onion and minced garlic, stirring occasionally, for about 6 minutes, until onion softens.
- Add broccoli, salt and ground pepper.
- Stir well.
- Add broth.
- Add almond milk.
- Bring to a simmer, cover and reduce heat to low.
- Cook, about 25 minutes, until broccoli is very tender.
- Transfer soup in batches to blender and puree until smooth.
- Return soup to the pan and stir in lemon juice.
- Heat and serve hot.

Turkey Soup

Ingredients for Stock Pot

1	Cooked turkey carcass (The remaining turkey and bones following a family dinner.)
2	3 in. Celery with leaves (not necessary to chop celery)
¼ cup	Chopped Onion
½ tsp	Salt
¼ tsp	Pepper
2	Bay Leaves

Directions for Stock Pot

- Remove most of the turkey from the bones. (Some turkey left on the bones gives added flavour.)
- Save the turkey from the bones to add to the turkey soup later.
- Remove fatty skin and other fat.
- Place bones in a large soup pot.
- Add water to mostly cover the bones.
- Add two bay leaves and the celery stalks (whole and with leaves), minced onion, salt and pepper.
- Bring water to a boil, then turn to simmer for 4 hours.
- Remove from heat and cool.

- Separate the turkey bones and meat from the liquid.
- Use strainer to ensure turkey broth is clear liquid.
- After separating, place turkey stock liquid in the refrigerator overnight.
- Clean turkey from the bones and refrigerate overnight.

Note: Chicken stock can be prepared using the same method as for turkey stock.

Turkey Soup Ingredients

4	*Carrots*
4	*Celery*
1	*medium Onion*
2	*Bay Leaves*
1 tsp	*Salt*
¼ tsp	*Pepper*
1 tsp	*Fresh Savoury*
½ tsp	*Garlic Powder*
½ tsp	*Sage*
1 cup	*Frozen Peas*
¼ cup	*Fresh Cauliflower*
¼ cup	*Fresh Broccoli*
1 cup	*Asparagus Water*
	Turkey Stock (Liquid made in the stock pot.)
	Turkey Pieces (Cooked in the stock pot.)

Directions

- Chop cleaned carrots, celery and onion. Cut cauliflower and broccoli into individual florets.
- Remove turkey stock from refrigerator.
- Skim off all the fat that rises to the top of the stock with a spoon and discard.
- Strain stock through a fine screen into a clean soup pot.
- Add all vegetables to the stock in the soup pot.
- Add bay leaves, salt, pepper, savoury, sage and garlic powder.
- Add 1 cup of asparagus water.
- Add cooked turkey pieces.
- Bring contents to a boil and then simmer for 2 hours.

Serve hot and enjoy!

Note: Vegetables and vegetable water can vary depending on what you have available. It is good to save vegetable water the day before making the soup. This adds flavour to the stock.

Leftover soup after cooling can be placed in containers and frozen for use later.

Turkey Soup

Green Bean Salad with Pecan Dressing

Ingredients

¾ lb	Green Beans
½ cup	Pecans
3 tbsp	Rice Vinegar
1 tbsp	Packed Fresh Dill
¼ tsp	Dijon Mustard
¼ tbsp	Minced Sweet Red Peppers

Directions

- Steam the beans until crisp – tender, about 3 – 4 minutes. Cool.
- Place the pecans, vinegar, dill and mustard in a blender. Process on low to medium speed until smooth, stopping frequently to scrape down the sides of the blender.
- Toss the beans with the pecan mixture and the minced peppers.

Enjoy!

3 Entrees

A Quick Method to Cook Fish Fillets
(Gluten Free)

Ingredients

6 to 8	*Fish Fillets (Your Choice of fish)*
1 Tbsp	*Water with 1 Tbsp of Flax Seed (This replaces 1 egg)*
¼ Cup	*Sugar Free Almond Milk*
1 Cup	*Crushed Rice Crackers*
1 Tbsp	*Olive Oil*
½ Tsp	*Salt*
¼ Tsp	*Pepper*
1	*Lemon*

Directions

- Cut whole lemon into narrow wedges.
- Wash fish fillets in water.
- Crush rice crackers.
- Wisk mixture of water and flax seed with almond milk, ½ tsp salt and ¼ tsp pepper.
- Place 1 tbsp of oil in frying pan.
- Dip the fish fillets in almond milk mixture, then cover with crushed rice crackers.
- Place fillets in oiled frying pan with medium heat.
- Turn fish over after 5 minutes.
- Cook for another 4 minutes, approximately.
- Fish is now ready.
- Serve with lemon wedges.

Enjoy!

Chili Con Carne

Ingredients

1 1/2 lb	*Ground Chicken (or ground beef if tolerated)*
2	*Large Onion*
1	*Green Sweet Pepper*
1 can	*Tomatoes (796 ml/28 fl oz)*
2 cans	*Red Kidney Beans (540 ml/19 fl oz per can)*
1 qt	*Water*
2 tsp	*Chili Powder*
½ tsp	*Salt*

Directions

- Brown onions in olive oil.
- Add ground chicken (or ground beef)
- Brown.
- Add other ingredients and simmer for 1 hour or until thick. (Could use a slow cooker to simmer)

Real Italian Spaghetti

In the first pot:

- Cook for 1 hour with lid on and medium heat:

10 oz	*Tomato Soup*
18 oz	*Tomato Paste*
20 oz	*Tomato Juice*
1	*Handful Parmesan Cheese*
1 Dash	*Sugar*
½ tbsp	*Ground Pepper*
2 tbsp	*Parsley*
½ tsp	*Oregano, poultry seasoning, sage, nutmeg, thyme, bay leaves*
2	*Bay Leaves*

(Half the amount or ¼ tsp of each of the above seasonings is enough, depending on your taste.)

In the second pot:

- Cook for 1 hour with medium heat:

¾ cup	*Olive Oil (cooking oil)*
1 lb	*Ground Pork*
1 lb	*Ground Beef*

- Brown meat thoroughly

Add:

2 Large	*Onions, sliced*
½ tsp	*Black Pepper*
½ tsp	*Salt*
1 cup	*Diced Celery*
2 cloves	*Garlic, blended*
7 Med.	*Mushrooms*

Combine the two pots:

- Cook for 2 hours, stirring occasionally

Double the recipe if desired.

The cooked sauce may be stored in bottles or plastic containers in the freezer.

Enjoy!

Salmon Loaf

Ingredients

1 lb	Can of Salmon
As required	Water or Almond Milk *
2 ½ tbsp	Ground Flax Seed mixed with 2 tbsp of water. Simmer to jell mixture together. (This replaces 1 egg.)
¾ cup	Plain rice crackers, crushed. Use salt free, if possible.
2 tsp	Lemon Juice
2 tsp	Onion, if desired
¼ tsp	Salt
1/8 tsp	Pepper
1	Lemon – cut into wedges

Directions

- Drain liquid from salmon into a measuring cup.
- *Add water or almond milk to make ¾ cup of liquid.
- Flake salmon, removing skin and skinny bones. Crush little round bones, placing in the flaked salmon. (Source of calcium.)
- Add lemon juice and stir.
- Blend in flaxseed mixture and remaining ingredients.
- Spoon lightly into a greased loaf pan or 1 qt baking dish.
- Bake: at 350F for 45 minutes.
- Serve with lemon wedges.

Shipwrecked Hash

Ingredients

1 tsp	Butter or Shortening
1	Medium Sized Onion, chopped
½ cup	Chopped Celery
1½ lb	Hamburg <u>or</u> 1½ lb Ground Chicken
½ cup	Precooked Rice
1 can	Tomato Soup (284 ml/10 fl oz)
1 can	Red Kidney Beans (540 ml/19 fl oz)
1 tbsp	Sugar
¼ tsp	Salt

Directions

- Melt butter, or shortening, in a pan on the stove.
- Brown onion and celery.
- Remove from element.
- Spread hamburg <u>or</u> ground chicken in the pan over the melted butter or shortening, browned onion and celery.
- Sprinkle with the pre-cooked rice.
- Add tomato soup, kidney beans and salt.
- Sprinkle on the sugar.
- Cook: at 350F for about 1 hour

Note: Pan can be a 1 ¼ qt pyrex casserole dish.

4 Desserts

Apple Crisp

Directions

- Peel and quarter 7 apples. Slice into an 8" x 8" glass dish or a casserole.
- Sprinkle with 2 tsp of lemon juice.
- Combine the following topping ingredients:

½ cup	Oat flour (or any flour that you can tolerate).
1/3 cup	Oatmeal
½ cup	Brown sugar <u>or</u> 4 tsp (2 packets) Stevia,
1/8 tsp	Salt
1 tsp	Cinnamon

- Stir well.
- Blend in with the pastry blender 1/8 cup butter or margarine.
- Spread mixture over the apples.
- Bake: 350F for 45 minutes, or until fruit is tender.

Peach Crisp

Directions

- Skin and slice 8 Peaches. Place them in a baking dish and sprinkle with a ¼ cup Water and 2 tsp Lemon Juice.

- Use the same topping ingredients as for Apple Crisp. Sprinkle over the Peaches.

- Bake: 350F for 45 minutes, or until fruit is tender.

Applesauce Cake
Egg Free & Dairy Free

Ingredients

2 cups	Applesauce
2 tsp	Baking Powder
1 tsp	Baking Soda
2 cups	Almond Flour
1 cup	Gluten Free All-Purpose Flour Blend
3 tbsp	Mashed Banana
5 tbsp	Virgin Oil
1 tbsp	Water

Directions

- Preheat oven to 325F.
- Mix flour, baking powder and baking soda in a bowl.
- In another bowl mix the applesauce, banana, oil and water.
- Add the liquid mixture to the flour mixture and mix.
- Place combined ingredients in an 8 in x 8 in greased square pan.
- Bake: 325F for about 40 minutes.

Applesauce Cake

Almond Butter Cookies

Ingredients

½ cup	Natural Almond Butter
½ cup	Maple Syrup (or ¼ cup Maple Syrup and ¼ cup Applesauce)
3 tbsp	Vegetable Oil
1 tsp	Vanilla Extract (or Almond Extract)
1 cup	Brown Rice Flour (or 1 cup all-purpose flour blend – Gluten Free)
½ tsp	Baking Soda
½ tsp	Salt
½ cup	Chopped Almonds (or Pecans if no Almonds available)

Directions

- Preheat oven to 350F.
- In a large bowl, combine natural almond butter, maple syrup, oil and vanilla extract until well blended.
- In a separate bowl, mix together brown rice flour, or 1 cup of all-purpose flour blend- Gluten Free, baking soda and salt.
- Add dry ingredients to wet ingredients, along with chopped almonds and stir until just combined.
- Let sit for 5 minutes.
- Roll heaping 1 tsp. of dough into balls.
- Flatten to about 1/3 inch and place onto a cookie sheet.

This cookie recipe can be doubled.

- Bake: 8 – 10 minutes.

Yield:

About 18 cookies

Banana Cookies

Ingredients

¾ cup	Brown Sugar (or ¾ cup Brown Splenda)
1 tbsp	Flax Seed
2 tbsp	Water
½ cup	Mashed Banana
½ tsp	Salt
2 cups	Gluten Free Flour Blend
½ tsp	Nutmeg
½ tsp	Baking Soda
2 tsp	Baking Powder
1 cup	Chopped Almonds

Directions

- Chop almonds in a chopper.
- Mash banana.
- Allow flax seed and water to sit for 2 minutes.
- Mix Brown sugar, or brown Splenda, with the flax seed and water mixture.
- Place gluten free flour blend in a bowl.
- Add to flour, nutmeg, baking soda, baking powder, salt and mix.
- Add chopped almonds to flour mixture.
- Add liquid to flour mixture.
- Drop by spoon onto a cookie sheet with parchment paper, or a greased cookie sheet.
- Bake: 400F for 15 minutes.
- Check cookies after 14 minutes with a toothpick or cake tester to ensure cookies are fully baked.

Baking time varies depending on your oven.

Oatmeal Carob Cookies

Twice as good the next day, if there are any left

Ingredients

1 cup	Margarine or shortening
¾ cup	Brown Sugar or use 1 ½ packets of Stevia in place of sugar.
½ cup	Applesauce
1 ½ cups	Oat Flour or a flour that is tolerated
1 tsp	Baking Soda
1 tsp	Salt
¾ cup	Carob Chips
2 cups	Quick Cooking Oatmeal
1 tsp	Vanilla
1 cup	Chopped Walnuts

Directions

- Cream margarine or shortening with Brown Sugar or Stevia. Add Applesauce and mix well.
- In another bowl, combine flour, sugar, baking soda and salt.
- Add these dry ingredients to the shortening mixture.
- Add remaining ingredients and stir well.
- Scoop out cookie dough about the size of a table soup spoon. Drop on a greased cookie sheet allowing a 1-inch space around each cookie.
- Bake: 375F for 8 to 10 minutes. Allow to cool.

Yield:

About 4 dozen

Pecan Puffs

Ingredients

1 cup	Margarine, _or_ 1 cup of Unsalted Butter
4 tbsp	Granulated Sugar, _or_ 2 (4 tsp) packets of Stevia
2 tsp	Vanilla
2 cups	Rice Flour
2 cups	Ground Pecans
½ tsp	Nutmeg
6 tsp	Water

Directions

- Cream margarine or butter until soft.
- Blend sugar or Stevia until creamy.
- Add vanilla and water.
- Stir flour, pecans and nutmeg into the mix.
- Roll dough into small balls.
- Place on greased pan.
- Bake: at 300F for about 45 minutes, or until done.

Enjoy!

White Chocolate Cookies with Cranberries

Ingredients

1 cup	250 ml	Amaranth Flour
¼ cup	60 ml	Tapioca Starch, or tapioca starch flour
½ tsp	2 ml	Baking Powder
½ tsp	2 ml	Baking Soda
¼ tsp	1 ml	Salt
¼ cup	60 ml	Pear Sauce
2/3 cup	133 ml	Margarine
½ cup	125 ml	Brown Sugar (or Stevia 1 ½ packets)
2 tbsp	8 ml	Water
1 tsp	4 ml	Vanilla Extract
1 cup	250 ml	Cooked Cranberries, drained, or Cranberry Crazens
1 cup	250 ml	Chopped White Chocolate

Directions

- In a bowl combine amaranth flour, tapioca starch, baking powder, baking soda and salt. Mix well and set aside.

- In a separate bowl, using an electric mixer, beat brown sugar, or Stevia, margarine, pear sauce, water, and vanilla until light and fluffy. Stir in cooked cranberries, draining liquid first, or cranberry crazens. Add white chocolate pieces to flour mixture and stir. Combine bowls.

- Drop dough by rounded spoonful 2 inches (5 cm) apart on lightly greased cookie sheets and flatten slightly. Bake immediately.

- Bake: 375F for about 12 - 14 minutes until lightly browned and just set.

- Let cool on baking sheets for 2 to 3 minutes.

- Carefully transfer to rack and let cool completely.

- Store in air tight container for 5 days or freeze for up to two months.

Note: Best to do one batch at a time.

White Chocolate Cookies with Cranberries

5 Miscellaneous

a. Gravy

b. Mashed Potatoes

c. Rice Stuffing

d. Roasted Almonds

Gravy
Gluten Free

Ingredients

1/4 cup	*Gluten Free all-purpose flour blend*
1/4 cup	*Water*
1 3/4 cup	*Vegetable Water*

Directions

- Remove meat from roasting pan.
- Place gluten free flour in roasting pan.
- Mix with water until smooth.
- Heat on stop of stove and add the vegetable water.
- Combine and stir until gravy bubbles. If consistency is too thick add ¼ cup of vegetable water.
- After cooking the potatoes, or other vegetables, drain and save the water to use in the gravy (or when making soup). The vegetable water adds extra flavour.

If more gravy is needed, simply double the recipe.

Mashed Potatoes

(Gluten Free)

Ingredients

5   Potatoes

Water or Sugar Free Almond Milk

Directions

- Peel potatoes and wash them.
- Cut potatoes in half.
- Cook in water in a pot on the stove for 15 minutes, or until soft.
- Mash potatoes with a potato masher, after draining potato water into a jar.
- Add a small amount (1/8 cup) of potato water or sugar free almond milk to the consistency of your choice.
- Serve hot with gravy, if desired.

Enjoy!

Rice Stuffing

Ingredients

1/3 cup	Rice
½ tsp	Salt
3 cups	Boiling Water
½ cup	Diced Celery
¼ cup	Diced Onion
1/3 cup	Olive Oil
5 ½ cups	Rice Krispies Cereal
2 tbsp	Mixed Parsley
½ tbsp	Poultry Seasoning
½ tsp	Savoury
½ cup	Poultry Stock or Water

Directions

- Wash rice thoroughly in a sieve and drain well.
- Add rice to salted boiling water 'slowly' so that the water continues to bubble.
- Boil rapidly 15 – 20 minutes until rice is tender.
- Drain in sieve.
- Brown celery and onion in olive oil.
- Stir in rice and mix well.
- Crush rice krispies into course crumbs
- Add parsley, seasonings and stock.
- Combine with rice and mix thoroughly.

Yield:

3 ½ cups (l cup required/lb of chicken or turkey.)

Note: Stuffing may be baked in a covered casserole in a moderate 375F oven for 25 minutes or baked in the breast cavity of a chicken or turkey.

Roasted Almonds

Ingredients

2 cups   Raw Almonds

Directions

- Place almonds in a single layer on a large cookie pan.
- Bake in a preheated oven at 275F for 30 minutes.
- After 25 minutes, remove 2 nuts from the pan, let cool and sample to see if they are done.
- The nuts can be kept in the oven at 275F for an additional 5 minutes, if needed.
- Remove pan from oven and let nuts cool before storing in a jar.

Note: For a whole bag of almonds, use 2 cookie pans, but always keep nuts in a single layer for heating.

Printed in the United States
By Bookmasters